THE! CREOLE ALMANACK

FOR

Trinidad & Tobago

1892

Printed by Anthony C. Blondel.

INDEX.

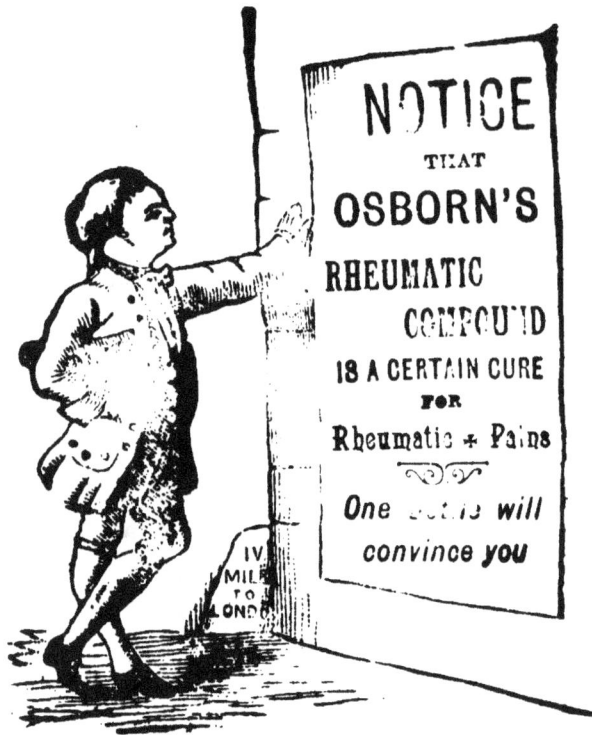

A Short Description of Trinidad and Tobago.

TRINIDAD.

TRINIDAD is the most southerly and the fifth largest of the West India Islands. It lies between Latitude 10° 4′ and 10° 50′ north and Longitude 60° 39′ and 62° west from Greenwich and contains an area of about 1,123,00 acres or 1,954 square miles. It was discovered by Christopher Colon in the year 1498 during his third voyage and named by him La Trinidad or The Trinity. It is situated very near the main land of Venezuela and almost opposite to one of the numerous mouths of the Orinoco. The island of Trinidad projects towards the mainland on the north and south forming an oblong and almost landlocked basin called the Gulf of Paria, affording a safe anchorage at all times for vessels of any size. There are four openings to this basin on the north, formed by three small islands which lie between the north-western end of Trinidad and the Venezuelan mainland and one opening on the south where the south-western end of Trinidad runs out towards the Delta of the Orinoco in the form of a cape. The openings on the north are called the Dragon's Mouths, and that on the south the Serpent's Mouth The Spanish for mouth is Boca and these openings are popularly known as the Bocas. A range of mountains which rise to the height of 3,000 feet above the sea runs along the northern side of the island and protect it from those severe hurricanes which sometimes sweep the Carribian Sea. The chief produce of Trinidad is Sugar, but Cocoa comes in a good second, the amount of Sugar shipped last year was 53,813 tons and of Cocoa 21,552,593 pounds, the other exports are Coconuts and Asphalt from the Pitch Lake, one of the wonders of the world. Only 350,000 acres of the Island are under cultivation or about one-fifth of its area.

The Sugar Cane is cultivated mostly on the plains running along the western side of the island, Cocoa in the valleys between the mountains on the northern side of the island, and Coconuts on the sandy shores of the eastern and southern sides of the Island.

Trinidad remained in the possession of the Spaniards until 1797 when it was taken by the English under Sir Ralph Abercrombie and has remained in their possession since then. It is governed as a Crown Colony by a Governor appointed by the Queen and a Legislative Council consisting of eight official members, heads of Departments, and eight unofficial members nominated by the Governor for four years, and eligible for re-nomination at the discretion of the Governor, who are supposed to represent particular districts of the Island.

Port-of-Spain, the capital of Trinidad, is situated on the Gulf of Paria, about nine miles from the northern openings or Bocas. Being built upon a gently sloping plain at the foot of a range of hills, it does not present an imposing appearance from the sea, only the buildings on the wharf being visible and a few small houses scattered on the hills behind the town, and strangers before they land have a very mean idea of the town, but when they land on the St. Vincent Jetty and proceeding along the wharf come to the foot of Marine Square, the size and beauty of the Town bursts upon them with a most agreeable surprise, and they find that although it looks from the deck of a ship as if the hills run down almost to the sea, in reality it is fully two miles from the wharf to the foot of the St. Ann's Hills, and that upon this gently sloping plain the town of Port-of-Spain is built. To the north of the town is a beautiful Savannah called the Queen's Park and in the town itself there are several squares, Brunswick Square, Marine Square, Tranquillity Square, and Harris' Square, there is also an open space to the east of the Eastern Market called Billiards' Orchard, although truth to tell there is not one tree on it. Port-of-Spain has about 27 miles of streets and 3,000 houses and covers an area of one square mile. Its population is 34,000 It is very decently lighted by kerosine oil lamps. Communication to the different parts of the town is by two lines of Tram Cars which run from the Railway Station on the South Quay to the eastern and western sides of the Queen's Park and by numerous cabs which can be hired at the rate of one shilling per mile or four shillings per hour. There are many nice buildings in the town such as t..e Roman Catholic and Anglican Cathedrals, the Sacred Heart Church, Greyfriars and St. John's Churches, All Saints' Church, the Police Buildings, the Colonial Hospital, and other private residences. Just outside the town in the Botanic Gardens is the Governor's residence, "St. Anne", a most noble pile. The scenery around the town is very pretty and there are several lovely valleys within easy walking distance of it among which may be mentioned the Belmont, St. Ann's, and Cascade Valleys, and a pleasant drive can be had to the Maraval Valley (where the chief reservoir which supplies the town with water is situated), the Santa Cruz Valley and the Diego Martin Valley.

Sanfernando, the second town of the Island, is situated on the Gulf of Paria about midway between Port-of-Spain and the south-western end of the Island. It is built on two low hills, and is the shipping port of most of the sugar from the Naparimas. Its population is seven thousand.

The third town is Arima situated 16 miles inland to the east of Port-of-Spain, and somewhat less than midway between the eastern and western coast of the Island. It is the terminus of one of the lines of railways (there are three lines in the Island) and the outlet of most of the Cocoa which is grown in the valleys to the north of it and on the rich lands which slope towards the east coast.

These three towns are municipalities. There is also the town of St. Joseph, the ancient Spanish capital of Trinidad, six miles to the east of Port-of-Spain along the railway line, and is the junction of the Arima and Sanfernando lines, this latter running along the shores of the Gulf between the two principal towns and is 30 miles long from the junction. The third line runs between Sanfernando and Princes Town, a rising town situated in the middle of the sugar district and the depôt for the cocoa plantations which are rapidly rising along the Mayaro trace which runs out to the south-eastern end of the Island. This line is 7 miles long. Communication between Sanfernando and the south-eastern end of the island is chiefly by steamers which ply tri-weekly. A steamer also runs weekly round the Island touching fortnightly at Tobago. The population of the whole island by the last census is 200,000.

~~~~~~~~~~~~~~~~~~~~~~~~~~~~

TOBAGO.

THE island of Tobago is situated to the north-east of Trinidad at a distance of about twenty miles. It is in 10° 9′ N. Lat. and 60° 12′ W. Long. It has an area of 114 square miles. Its greatest length is 26 miles and its breadth 7½ miles. It was discovered by Christopher Colon in 1498, and remained in the possession of the Spaniards till 1580 when it was taken by the British, it afterwards passed into the hands of the Dutch and French and finally in 1814 it was ceeded to the British. In the year 1889 it was united to Trinidad as one colony. Only about one-third of the Island is cultivated in sugar cane and provisions. Of late the cultivation of cocoa and coffee has been started, for which the climate and soil are admirably suited. The island is one of the most healthy of the West Indies. Scarborough, the capital, is situated at one end of a beautiful bay, which being however nearly surrounded by reefs, vessels of large tonnage cannot approach the anchorage except from one direction, (the south-westerly) coasting under the land until they reach the anchorage. The greater part of the town is built on an elevation overlooking the bay and the view from one or two points in it, or from the Fort is very beautiful. The situation of Scarborough is not however, the most desireable that can be conceived. It is said that the site was chosen for its stratagetic value. The population of the capital is 816. Plymouth, the former capital, has now dwindled down into a mean village, but its situation is preferable to that of Scarborough. It is built on a level plain and the streets (such as they are) are at right angles, while there is a beautiful and commodious harbour to the west of it. On the south-east of the island there is another splendid harbour called Man-of-War Bay, which it is said could accommodate the whole British Fleet. Tobago with abundant natural resources, is a very poor place. Already badly cultivated (only an outer fringe of the island having ever been under cultivation,) matters have been made worse by the disputes between the Proprietors and the Metayers (or tenants working the land on shares) culminating in numerous lawsuits in which the Proprietors have been every one heavily fined, and the consequence has been the abandonment of nearly all the Estates, only a few being now in a state of partial cultivation. The effect of this is terribly detrimental to Proprietors and Metayers alike. Lands lying waste, provide no support for the suffering labourers, while the Propritors themselves are most of them in a condition of dire impecuniosity. Education does not make the progress it ought. Schools are maintained by the various denominations, Anglican, Wesleyan, Moravian, and Roman Catholic; but not sufficient interest seems to be taken in the matter. The Government grants a small subsidy to each denomination but not sufficient means are available altogether to ensure efficiency. The Teachers are very badly paid, and they do, no doubt, the best they can, but inadequate remuneration must operate injuriously on their efforts. The Commerce of the island is in proportion to the lowness of the agriculture, there are eight stores in Scarborough and a few shops, these do their best to cater for the wants of the people. The stock they display is very creditable, but the returns are doubtless inadequate to the making of speedy fortunes. There is a very respectable Public Building, comprising Court Room and Government Offices, facing the Square. A newspaper entitled "The News" has just been started afresh, it having ceased to be issued for some time. It will be of service to the island if conducted with moderation and good temper, scurrillity being avoided. The population of Tobago is 18,000.

TIDES.

At full and new moon it is high water at Port-of-Spain, about half-past four o'clock, Spring Tides rise 4 feet, Neap Tides $2\frac{1}{2}$ feet. At the Bocas it is high water about half an hour before Port-of-Spain. At Sanfernando, La Brea and Oropouche from 8 to 15 minutes after Port-of-Spain.

J. A. RAPSEY,

Bread, Cake and Biscuit Baker,

DEALER IN

GROCERIES, PROVISIONS, WINES,

MALT LIQUORS,

AND

Family Supplies Generally.

————:o(:o:)o:————

Fresh Meats & Ice

Having lately enlarged his premises he is now prepared *to* attend to all orders from Town and Country with PROMPTNESS AND DESPATCH at

9, FREDERICK STREET,

Port-of-Spain.

AERATED WATER FACTORY,

Lemonade, Ginger Beer,

Orangeade and other Drinks.

OF BEST QUALITY AT MODERATE PRICE.

PRINCIPAL ARTICLES OF THE CALENDAR,
FOR THE YEAR 1892.

Golden Number	...	12	Dominical Letters	...	C.B.
Epact	... ...	1	Roman Indiction	...	5
Solar Cycle ...	...	25	Julian Period	...	6605

FIXED AND MOVABLE FESTIVALS, ANNIVERSARIES,
ETC., ETC., ETC.

Epiphany	... ... Jan. 6	Birth of Q. Victoria ... May 24
SEPTUAGESIMA SUNDAY Feby. 14		ASCENSION DAY—HOLY
SEXAGESIMA SUNDAY 21		THURSDAY 26
QUINQUAGESIMA—SHROVE		PENTECOST—WHIT SUNDAY
SUNDAY 28		June 5
St. David ... ... Mar. 1		TRINITY SUNDAY ... 12
ASH WEDNESDAY ... 2		CORPUS CHRISTI ... 16
QUADRAGESIMA—1ST SUNDAY		Accession of Q. Victoria 20
IN LENT 6		St. John Baptist ... 24
St. Patrick 17		St. Michael—Michaelmas
Annunciation—Lady Day 25		Day Sept. 29
PALM SUNDAY ... April 10		Birth of Prince of Wales Nov 9
GOOD FRIDAY ... 15		1ST SUNDAY IN ADVENT 27
EASTER SUNDAY ... 17		St. Andrew ... 30
St. George 23		St. Thomas ... ... Dec. 21
LOW SUNDAY ... 24		Christmas Day ... 25
ROGATION SUNDAY ... May 22		

The Year 5653 of the Jewish Era commences on September 22, 1892.

Ramadân (Month of Abstinence) observed by the Turks commences on March 30, 1892.

The Year 1310 of the Mohammedan Era commences on July 26, 1892.

JANUARY 1892.

Days of Month.	Days of Week.		D.	H.	M.
		First Quarter	6	5	20 p.m.
		Full Moon	13	7	30 p.m.
		Last Quarter	21	7	50 p.m.
		New Moon	29	8	46 p.m.

Days of Month.	Days of Week.	
1	F	*Public Holiday*—Tobago and Trinidad united
2	S	(1) Sunday Closing Ordinance enforced 1882
3	Sun	*2nd Sunday after Christmas*
4	M	
5	Tu	Appeal Court
6	W	PACKET DUE—Borough Council meets
7	Th	Princes Albert and George of Wales visited Trinidad 1880
8	F	(7) Supreme Court, Summary Jurisdiction (San Fernando)
9	S	
10	Sun	*1st Sunday after Epiphany*
11	M	
12	Tu	
13	W	D'Azevedo's Fire 1885
14	Th	PACKET LEAVES
15	F	Supreme Court Summary Jurisdiction
16	S	(15) Reform meeting 1887
17	Sun	*2nd Sunday after Epiphany*
18	M	
19	Tu	Appeal Court
20	W	PACKET DUE—Borough Council meets
21	Th	Greyfriars Church (Presbyterian) opened 1839
22	F	
23	S	(24) John Scott Bushe died 1887
24	Sun	*3rd Sunday after Epiphany*
25	M	Lord Harris left 1854
26	Tu	
27	W	Great Fire in Port-of-Spain 1884—damages £41,000
28	T	PACKET LEAVES
29	F	(28) Railway Collision 1885 (Champ Fleures)
30	S	St. John's Church (Baptist) opened 1845
31	Sun	*4th Sunday after Epiphany*

Fruits ripe—Pomarak, Water Melons, Orange, Tamarinds.

FEBRUARY 1892.

Days of Month.	Days of Week.				
			D.	H.	M.
		First Quarter	5	1	47 a.m.
		Full Moon	12	11	46 a.m.
		Last Quarter	20	0	22 p.m.
		New Moon	27	7	55 p.m.

1	M	Legislative Council meets
2	Tu	Appeal Court
3	W	PACKET DUE—Borough Council meets
4	Th	Criminal Sessions—San Fernando
5	F	Supreme Court Summary Jurisdiction
6	S	
7	Sun	*5th Sunday after Epiphany*
8	M	
9	Tu	Criminal Sessions—Port-of-Spain
10	W	
11	Th	PACKET LEAVES
12	F	
13	S	Fire in Charlotte Street 1891
14	Sun	*Septuagesima Sunday*—St. Valentine's Day.
15	M	Fire in Marine Square 1891. 11 lives lost
16	Tu	Appeal Court.—R. C. Presbytery opened 1880
17	W	PACKET DUE.—Borough Council meets
18	Th	
19	F	Supreme Court Summary Jurisdiction
20	S	
21	Sun	*Sexagesima Sunday.*—Cannes Boulay disturbance 1881.
22	M	
23	Tu	Exhibition in Port-of-Spain 1886
24	W	Cannes Boulay abolished 1884,
25	Th	PACKET LEAVES.
26	F	Charles Warner died 1889.
27	S	
28	Sun	*Quinquagesima Sunday*
29	M	

Fruits Ripe :—Sapodilla, Mamesapote, Cashew, Tamarind.

MUIR, MARSHALL & Co.,
The West End Store,
13a, Chacon Street,—Port-of-Spain.

DEPÔT FOR

TOYS, Fancy Goods, School Books and School Stationery Office, General and Fancy Stationery—Artists' Materials—Printers' and Bookbinders' Sundries—Terra Cotta Goods—Cheap Music, French Novels—Spanish Novels—Prayer and Hymn Books for all Denominations—Church Services—Reward Books—Books for presentations and prizes—Children's Picture Books—School Wall Maps—Admiralty Charts—Sundries for Engineers and Draughtsmen—Waterbury Watches—Teachers Bibles—Family Bibles, etc., etc., etc.

A complete assortment of works by Standard English Novelists and Standard Poets.   Latest Novels received from England and America as published

Agents for the Sale of the " British and Foreign Bible Society's " Bibles.

We beg specially to call the attention of Shippers, Merchants' Estates Proprietors and School Managers to our varied stock of

Ledgers, Day Books, Journals,

Cash Books, Hospital Case Books, Field Books, Memorandum Books, Estate Labour Books, &c., comprising as it does *the largest and most select stock of the kind in the West Indies.*

CUSTOMS FORMS

AND

Government Vouchers kept in Stock,

Calling Cards printed on the premises on the shortest notice and in neatest and most fashionable styles.

MARCH 1892.

Days of Month.	Days of Week,				
			D.	H.	M.
		First Quarter	5	11	22 a.m.
		Full Moon	13	5	1 a.m.
		Last Quarter	21	9	24 a.m.
		New Moon	28	5	25 a.m.

1	Tu	Shrove Tuesday.—Legislative Council.—Appeal Court
2	W	ASH WEDNESDAY.—PACKET DUE.—Boro' Council Meets
3	Th	Supreme Court Summary Jurisdiction (Sanfernando)
4	F	Supreme Court Summary Jurisdiction
5	S	Fire in Port-of-Spain 1887 ; damages £35,000
6	Sun	*First Sunday in Lent*
7	M	
8	Tu	
9	W	
10	Th	PACKET LEAVES.—Governor Elliott arrived 1854
11	F	
12	S	
13	Sun	*Second Sunday in Lent.*—Archbishop Gonin died 1889.
14	M	
15	Tu	Appeal Court
16	W	PACKET DUE—Borough Council Meets
17	Th	
18	F	Supreme Court Summary Jurisdiction
19	S	
20	Sun	*Third Sunday in Lent*
21	M	
22	Tu	
23	W	
24	Th	PACKET LEAVES.—Port-of-Spain destroyed by fire 1808
25	F	Lady Day,—Trinity Cathedral consecrated 1823
26	S	Roman Catholic Cathedral commenced 1816
27	Sun	*Fourth Sunday in Lent.*—Sir F. Freeling left 1884
28	M	
29	Tu	
30	W	PACKET DUE.—Borough Council meets
31	Th	House and Land Tax Due

Fruits Ripe :—Orange, Star Apple, Mamesapote, Cashew, Shaddock.

APRIL 1892.

			D.	H,	M.
First Quarter			3	10	29 p.m.
Full Moon			11	10	34 p.m.
Last Quarter			19	10	4 p.m.
New Moon			26	1	54 p.m.

Days of Month	Days of Week	
1	F.	Legislative Council.—Supreme Court Summary Jurisdict'n
2	S	
3	Sun	*Fifth Sunday in Lent*
4	M	
5	Tu	Appeal Court
6	W	Old Lady Day
7	Th	PACKET LEAVES.—Criminal Sessions Sanfernando
8	F	
9	S	
10	Sun	*Palm Sunday*
11	M	
12	Tu	Criminal Sessions Port-of-Spain
13	W	PACKET DUE.—Borough Council meets
14	Th	
15	F	*Good Friday.*—Public Holiday
16	S	(15) Roman Catholic Cathedral consecrated 1832
17	Sun	*Easter Sunday.*—Sanfernando Railway opened 1882,
18	M	Public Holiday.—Trinity Church chimes first rung 1881
19	Tu	Appeal Court
20	W	
21	Th	PACKET LEAVES
22	F	Demerara taken 1796
23	S	St. George
24	Sun	*Low Sunday*
25	M	
26	Tu	
27	W	PACKET DUE,—Borough Council meets
28	Th	Lord Harris arrived 1846
29	F	
30	S	

Fruits Ripe :—Orange, Cashew, Mamesapote, Pine Apple.

W. C. ROSS,

Chemist and Druggist,

Colonial Dispensary,

2, FREDERICK STREET,

PORT-OF-SPAIN,—TRINIDAD

Prescriptions accurately Prepared,

Copied and Returned.

Every Article of the Best Description.

Physicians prescriptions and Family Recipes carefully dispensed by competent Licensed Druggists with the Choicest Drugs.

Family and Sea Medicine Chests

Fitted up with Appropriate Medicines and Directions fer every Climate.

NIGHT BELL.

2, Frederick Street.

MAY 1892.

Days of Month.	Days of Week.				
			D.	H.	M.
		First Quarter	3	11	19 a.m.
		Full Moon	11	3	7 p.m.
		Last Quarter	19	7	0 a.m.
		New Moon	25	1	57 a.m.

1	Sun	*Second Sunday after Easter*
2	M	Legislative Council meets
3	Tu	Appeal Court
4	W	Rosary Chapel opened 1867
5	Th	PACKET LEAVES.—Supreme Court Sum. Jur. (Sanfernndo)
6	F	Supreme Court Summary Jurisdiction (Port-of-Spain)
7	S	
8	Sun	*Third Sunday after Easter*
9	M	(8) First Loan Meeting of Trin. B. and L. Association 1891
10	Tu	(9) Sacred Heart Church commenced 1880
11	W	PACKET DUE.—Borough Council meets
12	Th	(11) Bishop Rawle died 1889.
13	F	
14	S	
15	Sun	*Fourth Sunday after Easter*
16	M	(15) Colonial Bank opened 1837
17	Tu	Appeal Court.—Bishop Hayes arrived 1889.
18	W	
19	Th	PACKET LEAVES
20	F	Supreme Court Summary Jurisdiction
21	S	
22	Sun	*Rogation Sunday*
23	M	
24	Tu	Queen's Birthday—Public Holiday
25	W	PACKET DUE.—Borough Council meets
26	Th	ASCENSION DAY
27	F	
28	S	
29	Sun	*Sunday after Ascension*
30	M	Trinity Church commenced 1816
31	Tu	(30) Coolies first introduced 1845

Fruits Ripe : Sapodilla, Orange, Pine Apple, Cashew, Custard Apple

JUNE 1892.

		D. H, M.
		First Quarter 2 1 59 a.m.
		Full Moon 10 5 40 a.m.
		Last Quarter 17 1 8 p.m.
		New Moon 24 6 14 a.m.

Days of Month.	Days of Week	
1	W	Legislative Council
2	Th	PACKET LEAVES.—Criminal Sessions Sanfernando
3	F	Supreme Court Summary Jurisdiction.
4	S	Wet Season began 1877
5	Sun	*Whit Sunday*
6	M	Public Holiday
7	Tu	Appeal Court
8	W	PACKET DUE.—Borough Council meets
9	Th	
10	F	
11	S	St. James Barracks finished 1827
12	Sun	*Trinity Sunday*
13	M	
14	Tu	Criminal Sessions Port-of-Spain
15	W	
16	Th	PACKET LEAVES.—Corpus Christi—Public Holiday
17	F	Supreme Court Summary Jurisdiction
18	S	Mutiny of Black Troops 1837
19	Sun	*First Sunday after Trinity*
20	M	Jubilee of Queen Victoria's Accession 1837.
21	Tu	Appeal Court
22	W	PACKET DUE,—Borough Council meets
23	Th	Railway collision 1881, Covua line
24	F	
25	S	Governor Gordon left 1870
26	Sun	*Second Sunday after Trinity*
27	M	(26) First hogshead of sugar carried on Cipero Tramway '31
28	Tu	Model Schools vacation begins
29	W	
30	Th	PACKET LEAVES.—Maxwell Philip died 1888.

Fruits Ripe :—Mango, Tamarind, Cashew, Pine Apple, Sadpodilla, Pomarak.

JULY 1892.

			D.	H.	M.
		First Quarter	1	6	21 p.m.
		Full Moon	9	5	51 p.m.
		Last Quarter	16	5	55 p.m.
		New Moon	23	3	38 p.m.
		First Quarter	31	11	53 a.m.

Days of Month.	Days of Week.	
1	F	Legislative Council meets—Sup. Court Sum. Jurisdiction
2	S	Vacation Public Schools begins
3	Sun	*Third Sunday after Trinity*
4	M	(3) Governor Rennie arrived 1872
5	Tu	Appeal Court
6	W	PACKET DUE—Borough Council meets
7	Th	Supreme Court, Summary Jurisdiction (San Fernando)
8	F	
9	S	
10	Sun	*Fourth Sunday after Trinity*
11	M	
12	Tu	
13	W	
14	Th	PACKET LEAVES
15	F	St. Swithin's Day—Supreme Court, Summary Jurisdiction
16	S	
17	Sun	*Fifth Sunday after Trinity*
18	M	
19	Tu	Appeal Court
20	W	PACKET DUE—Borough Council meets
21	Th	
22	F	
23	S	
24	Sun	*Sixth Sunday after Trinity*
25	M	(24) Governor's Palace, St. Anne, commenced 1873
26	Tu	
27	W	
28	T	PACKET LEAVES
29	F	
30	S	Sir William Robinson left 1891
31	Sun	*Seventh Sunday after Trinity.*—Trinidad Discovered 1498

Fruits ripe—Mango, Sapodilla, Pomarak, Sugar Apple, Soursop.

The "Bee-hive,"

St. Vincent Street,

Midway between the Royal Mail Company's Office, and the
Post Office.

Photography!   Photography!!

The undersigned begs to inform his friends and the public
generally that he is always receiving supplies of

Fresh Photographic Materials AND CHEMICALS
of the very best quality—such as Gun Cotton, Nitrate of Silver,
Cloride of Gold, Hypo. Alum, Oxalate of Potash, Sulphite of
Soda, Sulphate of Iron, &c., &c.

Dry Plates FROM THE VERY BEST MAKERS, AND
at the lowest rates.

Portrait Albums A LARGE AND TASTY ASSORT-
ment from 60 cents upwards each.

Birthday Cards A LARGE AND VARIED ASSORT-
ment to suit all tastes and purses.

Sensitized Paper AMATEURS WHO HAVE NOT THE
skill, time and inclination or appliances to sensitize their paper
preparatory to printing, are reminded that such can be obtained
daily at the "Bee-hive" of the finest quality and uniform sensi-
tiveness. Sent to any address on receipt of 40 cents per sheet
which includes postage.

Photo Views of Trinidad THESE ARE A
Speciality, and the public are respectfully invited to examine
his stock before purchasing elsewhere.

Portraits HE STILL CONTINUES TO TAKE PHOTOS,
in every style, Wedding and Family Groups, taken at their residences and Photos of the Dead, Estates and Private Residences,

AT THE SHORTEST NOTICE AND MOST MODERATE RATES,
Telephone 111.   W. K. WILLIAMSON.

*Beware of cheap Photos which will not last, but fade after a short
time.*

AUGUST 1892.

			D.	H.	M.
Full Moon			8	4	5 a.m.
Last Quarter			14	10	45 p.m.
New Moon			22	3	6 a.m.
First Quarter			30	4	36 a.m.

Days of Month.	Days of Week.	
1	M	Legislative Council meets
2	Tu	Appeal Court—Bishop Rawle arrived 1871
3	W	PACKET DUE—Borough Council meets
4	Th	Supreme Court, Summary Jurisdiction—San Fernando
5	F	Supreme Court Summary Jurisdiction—Port-of-Spain
6	S	
7	Sun	*Eighth Sunday after Trinity*
8	M	
9	Tu	
10	W	
11	Th	PACKET LEAVES,—Hurricane in Trinidad 1810
12	F	
13	S	First Book printed 1457—Trade and Taxes Commission 1886
14	Sun	*Ninth Sunday after Trinity*
15	M	
16	Tu	Appeal Court
17	W	PACKET DUE.—Borough Council meets
18	Th	(17) Charter of Arima Borough granted 1887
19	F	Governor Sir Napier Broome arrived 1891
20	S	Great Fire in Sanfernando 1882
21	Sun	*Tenth Sunday after Trinity*
22	M	
23	Tu	
24	W	
25	Th	PACKET LEAVES.
26	F	
27	S	
28	Sun	*Eleventh Sunday after Trinity.*—Slavery abolished 1833
29	M	
30	Tu	Cholera broke out in Trinidad '54.—Arima Ralway op'd '76
31	W	PACKET DUE.—Borough Council meets

Fruits Ripe :—Avacado, Sugar Apple, Guava, Orange, Govnr. Plum.

C. L. HALEY & CO.,

47 and 48, King Street, Port-of-Spain,

TRINIDAD.

Commission Merchants,

AND DEALERS IN

Ice, Fresh Meats, Liquors, Groceries,

AND

FAMILY SUPPLIES GENERALLY.

Wholeasle or Retail, in Bond or duty paid.

Ship Stores Supplied on the Shortest Notice.

THE FAMILY HOTEL,

47, KING STREET,

Port-of-Spain, Trinidad.

This Hotel has been started by the Proprietors of the Ice Establishment to add to the accommodation which already existed at No. 48 for gentlemen only, a respectable, roomy, airy, comfortable and

WELL FURNISHED HOTEL,

With Bath and every necessary requisite; every room provided with its electric bell, where whole families can be accommodated, and where genlemen or ladies, with or without families, may find the comforts of a quiet home. Rooms may be taken, and arrangements made for Board and Lodging, for a month or for longer or shorter periods.

ACCOMMODATION OF THE BEST AND AT MODERATE PRICES.

C. L. HALEY & CO., Proprietors.

SEPTEMBER 1892.

Days of Month.	Days of Week				
			D.	H,	M.
		Full Moon	6	1	15 p.m.
		Last Quarter	13	4	57 a.m.
		New Moon	20	5	24 p.m.
		First Quarter	28	10	27 p.m.

1	Th	Legislative Council meets
2	F	(1) Telegraphic Cable laid to Trinidad 1875
3	S	"Port-of-Spain Gazette" first published 1825
4	Sun	*Twelfth Sunday after Trinity*
5	M	
6	Tu	Appeal Court
7	W	
8	Th	PACKET LEAVES
9	F	Battle of Kassassin 1882
10	S	
11	Sun	*Thirteenth Sunday after Trinity*
12	M	
13	Tu	Battle of Tel-el-Kebir 1882
14	W	PACKET DUE.—Borough Council meets
15	Th	
16	F	
17	S	Judge Knox died 1869
18	Sun	*Fourteenth Sunday after Trinity*
19	M	Severe Earthquake in 1825
20	Tu	Appeal Court
21	W	
22	Th	PACKET LEAVES
23	F	
24	S	Governor Gordon left 1870
25	Sun	*Fifteenth Sunday after Trinity*
26	M	
27	Tu	
28	W	PACKET DUE.—Borough Council meets
29	Th	Michaelmas Day
30	F	Last day for paying Water Rates

Fruits Ripe:—Pomme Cythere, Governor Plum, Avocado, China Plum

THE "CARLISLE,"

No. 2, St. Vincent Street,

PORT-OF-SPAIN,

OFFERS ALL THE ADVANTAGES OF A

FIRST CLASS ESTABLISHMENT,

Having two Cool and SPACIOUS DINING SALOONS, in which we guarantee the best of accommodation and first class attention, and a

B A R

Always stocked with the Choicest Wines and Spirits,

AND A LARGE ASSORTMENT OF

Havana Cigars, Cigarettes, Pipes, etc. ;

IN ADDITION

A BILLIARD SALOON,

Built specially for the late Colonial Club and admitted by all to be the largest and coolest in Trinidad.

The "CARLISLE" being in close proximity with all the principal offices, and the Tram Cars passing its doors every ten minutes, visitors can avail themselves of the convenience of a comfortable resort.

☞ *Breakfast supplied monthly at reasonable rates.*

ALSO.

A GROCERY ESTABLISMENT,

Which is stocked with goods from English and American markets, to be sold at prices to suit the times.

CRONEY & CO.

OCTOBER 1892.

		D.	H.	M.
Full Moon		5	10	19 p.m.
Last Quarter		12	1	45 p.m.
New Moon		20	10	32 a.m.
First Quarter		28	1	34 a.m.

Days of Month.	Days of Week.	
1	S	Legislative Council meets
2	Sun	*Sixteenth Sunday after Trinity*
3	M	
4	Tu	Appeal Court
5	W	
6	Th	PACKET LEAVES.—Criminal Sessions Sanfernando
7	F	Supreme Court Summary Jurisdiction
8	S	Bishop Hyland died 1884
9	Sun	*Seventeenth Sunday after Trinity*
10	M	Trial by Jury introduced 1844
11	Tu	Criminal Sessions Port-of-Spain
12	W	PACKET DUE—Borough Council meets
13	Th	
14	F	Battle of Hastings 1066
15	S	
16	Sun	*Eighteenth Sunday after Trinity*
17	M	
18	Tu	Appeal Court
19	W	
20	Th	PACKET LEAVES.
21	F	Supreme Court Summary Jurisdiction
22	S	
23	Sun	*Nineteenth Sunday after Trinity*
24	M	
25	Tu	Battle of Agincourt 1415
26	W	PACKET DUE.—Borough Council meets
27	Th	
28	F	Exhibition at Prince's Building opened 1890
29	S	
30	Sun	*Twentieth Sunday after Trinity*—Coolie Hosein, dis'nce '84
31	M	All Hollows Eve

Fruits Ripe :—Avacado, Pomme Cythere, Jamaica Plum, Soursop, Sapodilla.

NOVEMBER 1892.

			D.	H.	M.
		Full Moon	4	7	57 a.m.
		Last Quarter	11	2	9 a.m.
		New Moon	19	5	27 a.m.
		First Quarter	27	2	35 a.m.

Days of Month.	Days of Week.	
1	Tu	Legislative Council meets—Appeal Court—Boro' Elections
2	W	(1) All Saints' Day
3	Th	PACKET LEAVES.—Supreme Court Sum. Jur. (Sanfernndo)
4	F	Supreme Court Summary Jurisdiction (Port-of-Spain)
5	S	(4) Police Buildings burnt down 1881
6	Sun	*Twenty-first Sunday after Trinity*
7	M	
8	Tu	
9	W	PACKET DUE.—Borough Council meets
10	Th	
11	F	Martinmass.—Wesleyan Chapel (Hanover-st.) opened 1827
12	S	
13	Sun	*Twenty-sceond Sunday after Trinity*
14	M	Trinidad Volunteers instituted 1878
15	Tu	Appeal Court
16	W	
17	Th	PACKET LEAVES
18	F	Supreme Court Summary Jurisdiction
19	S	
20	Sun	*Twenty-third Sunday after Trinity*
21	M	(20) Governor Irving arrived 1874
22	Tu	
23	W	PACKET DUE.—Borough Council meets
24	Th	
25	F	
26	S	
27	Sun	*Advent Sunday*
28	M	
29	Tu	Assessment Returns to be sent in.
30	W	St. Andrew's Day

Fruits Ripe : Orange, Guava, Sapodilla, Sugar Apple, Pomme Cythere

DECEMBER 1892.

			D.	H.	M.
		Full Moon	3	6	25 p.m.
		Last Quarter	10	6	37 p.m.
		New Moon	19	0	21 a.m.
		First Quarter	26	1	30 p.m.

Days of Month.	Days of Week.	
1	Th	Legislative Council meets—Criminal Sessions, Sanfernando
2	F	Supreme Court Summary Jurisdiction
3	S	Sacred Heart Church opened 1882
4	Sun	*Second Snnday in Advent*
5	M	
6	Tu	Appeal Court
7	W	PACKET DUE—Borough Council meets
8	Th	
9	F	
10	S	Royal Academy founded 1768
11	Sun	*Third Sunday in Advent*
12	M	
13	Tu	Criminal Sessions, Port-of-Spain
14	W	
15	Th	PACKET LEAVES
16	F	Supreme Court Summary Jurisdiction
17	S	
18	Sun	*Fourth Snnday in Advent*
19	M	
20	Tu	Appeal Court.—First steamer plied in Gulf 1818
21	W	PACKET DUE—Borough Council meets
22	Th	
23	F	Prince Consort buried 1861
24	S	
25	Sun	CHRISTMAS DAY
26	M	First cargo of ice landed in Trinidad 1844—Public Holiday
27	Tu	Innocents' Day
28	W	
29	T	PACKET LEAVES
30	F	
31	S	Toll Gate abolished 1878,

Fruits ripe—Mango, Guava, Avocado, Sapodilla, Melons

POSTAL REGULATIONS, INLAND.

THE General Post Office in St. Vincent Street Port-of-Spain is open daily for the despatch of ordinary business at from 7 a.m. to 4 p.m. Sundays and Public Holidays excepted, when the hours are from 7 to 8 a.m. There are three house-to-house deliveries of letters in Port-of-Spain every day (except Sundays and Public Holidays) at 7 and 10 a.m. and 2 p.m. On the day the English Packet mails are received only one house to house delivery is made of Inland letters only.

INLAND RATES.—Letters not exceeding ½ oz. 1d. Every additional ½ oz. or part thereof 1d. For every newspaper, circular or prices current not exceeding 4 ozs. ½d For every packet of 2 or more newspapers, &c., not exceeding 4 ozs. ½d., for every additional 4 ozs. or part thereof 1d. For any book packet not exceeding 2 ozs. ½d., every additional 2 oz. or part of it ½d. No letter, newspaper or book packet to exceed 2 ℔s. in weight and 18 x 9 inches in dimension.

POST CARD.—Nothing besides the address must be written or printed on the face of a Post Card, nor must it be cut or folded, neither should anything be attached to the card. If any of these rules are infringed the card will be charged 1d. on delivery.

REGISTRATION.—The fee for registering a letter, newspaper, or book-packet is 2d. and the registration fee, and the postage must be prepaid. No article addressed to initials or to a fictitious name can be registered unless it be addressed to the care of a person or Firm. Every article presented for registration must be enclosed in a strong cover, securely fastened. Every article to be registered must be given to an agent of the Post Office and a receipt obtained for it. If contrary to this rule an article be dropped into a letter box marked *registered*, it would be liable to a fee of 8d. if directed to any place in the Island instead of the ordinary fee of 2d. Letters or Packets containing Watches, Coin, or Jewellery if posted without registration are subjected to a registration and are charged on delivery 8d. in addition to the ordinary postage. No letters containing coin are accepted for registration to any place outside the colony.

Jno. Geo. D'Ade & Co.

NO. 15, FREDERICK STREET, PORT-OF-SPAIN.

IMPORTERS OF

DRY GOODS,

English, American & Austrian Furniture,

ENGLISH AND AMERICAN

ELECTRO PLATED WARE.

SADDLERY & HARNESS.

LAWN TENNIS BATS & BALLS, &c.

CRICKETING REQUISITES, VIZ: BATS, BALLS, STUMPS, BATTING AND WICKET KEEPING GLOVES. ALSO THE CELEBRATED KNEE PADS, "MAGIC" BAT

BANNISTER BRUSHES, HOUSE & STABLE BROOMS.

Hair, Fibre and Straw Mattresses

Made by experienced workmen at the shortest notice

AGENTS FOR CHOCOLAT MENIER.

AGENTS FOR THE

"ORMONDE" SAFETY BICYCLES.

Luce's Celebrated Eau-de-Cologne.

Molliscorium & Stevens's "Silicon."

PARCEL POST (INLAND).

1. No parcel may be more than 3 feet 6 inches long or 6 feet in length and girth combined. To places in class A. no parcel may exceed 11 pounds and in places in class B. 4 pounds in weight.

2. Post Offices in class A. are Port-of-Spain, San Fernando, Arima, California, Caroni, Chaguanas, Claxton Bay, Couva, Cedros, Conupia, Dabadie, Diego Martin, Irois, LaBrea, Mucurapo, Monos, Princes Town, St. Joseph, Tumpura, Tunapuna and Williamsville.

3. Post offices in Class B. are Arouca, Blanchisseuse, Chatham, Erin, Gran Couva, Hicacos, Manzanilla, Maraval, Moruga, Mayaro, Oropouche, Santa Cruz, St. Ann's, San Juan, Tacarigua, St. Madelaine, Tortuga and Toco.

4. Rates of Postage—of Parcels not exceeding 1 ℔. 3 pence. For every additional pound or part thereof 1½d.

5. Parcels must be taken to the post office between the hours of 10 a.m. and 4 p.m. and handed to the officer appointed to receive them and should not be left until they have been weighed and the necessary postage affixed on them and a receipt obtained for them.

6. Parcels should be plainly directed and the words "Parcel Post" written on the left hand upper corner.

7. It is prohibited to forward parcels which contain Letters, Ice, Gunpowder, Cartridges, Matches, Explosive-substances, Bladders containing liquids, Live Animals, grossly offensive or filthy matter, or anything in a condition likely to injure other parcels or any officer of the Post Office.

8. Parcels should be so packed as to guard against injury to other parcels, especially liquids or semi-liquids which must be in well corked cases or bottles, packed so as to prevent breakage.

PARCEL POST—FOREIGN.

PARCELS subject to the above regulations will be received for transmission to the United Kingdom up to 4 p.m. on the day before the departure of the English mail, at all Post Offices in class A. At offices in class B. the parcels must be posted 30 minutes before the closing of the mail and in time for them to arrive in Port-of-Spain before 4 p.m. on the day before the English mail leaves.

DSEPATCH OF INLAND MAILS.

DISPATCHED FROM	FOR
Port-of-Spain ...	Diego Martin—Daily at 2.45 p.m.
,, ...	Maraval and St. Ann's— Daily at 9.45 a.m.
,, ...	*St. Juan, St. Joseph, Tacarigua, Arouca, Dabadie and Arima—Daily at 8 a.m., 1.30 and 3.45 p.m.
,, ...	*Caroni, Conupia, Chaguanas, Carapichaima, Savonetta, Couva, Claxton Bay, San Fernando, Williamsville & Princes Town...Daily at 6.30 and 10.30 a.m. and 3.30 p.m.
,, ...	Oropouche, Capdeville, La Brea, Irois, Cedros and Icacos—MONDAYS and SATURDAYS 6.30 a.m. TUESDAYS 3.15 p.m.
,, ...	Mayaro and Manzanilla—WEDNESDAYS & SATURDAYS 3.45 p.m.
,. ...	Carenage, The Islands and Monos—MONDAYS 1.30 p.m., WEDNESDAYS 7.30 a.m. FRIDAYS 2.30 p.m., SATURDAYS 12.30 p.m.
,, ...	*Santa Cruz Daily at 8 a.m. & 3.30 p.m.
,, ...	†Blanchisseuse—SATURDAY at 8 a. m.
,, ...	†Toco—MONDAYS and THURSDAYS at 8 a. m.
,, ...	*Tumpuna—TUESDAYS and THURSDAYS.
,, ...	†Moruga—TUESDAYS and THURSDAYS.
Maraval ...	Port-of-Spain, &c.—Daily at 1.30 p. m.
St. Ann's ...	,, 2.30 ,,
San Fernando }	La Brea, Cedros and Oropouche—MONDAYS and SATURDAYS at 9 a.m., WEDNESDAYS 6.30 a. m.
San Fernando ...	Princes Town and Williamsville—Twice Daily
Diego Martin St. James and Cocorite }	Port-of-Spain, &c.—Due at G. P, O. 10 a.m.
Icacos, Cedros, &c.	Port-of-Spain and San Fernando, &c.—MONDAYS, WEDNESDAYS and SATURDAYS.
Gran Couva & Montserrat }	Couva—Daily.
Mayaro, Nariva Manzanilla & Sangre Grande }	Port-of-Spain, &c.—Tuesdays and Fridays.

* *Return Mails made up on same days and hours.*
† ,, ,, ,, *the day after.*

Mails are also dispatched by the Fruit Steamers which go round the Island leaving Port-of-Spain every alternate Tuesday and returning on the following Saturday.

G. DONAWA & Co.,

SAN FERNANDO, TRINIDAD,

Fancy and General Drapers,

Hatters, Clothiers,

Boot and Shoe Merchants

AND

General Warehousemen.

AN EXTENSIVE AND COMPLETE

ASSORTMENT OF GOODS

ALWAYS ON HAND

☞ NEW ARRIVALS BY ALMOST EVERY STEAMER.

HIGH-CLASS TAILORING

A SPECIALITY.

SUITS MADE TO ORDER ON THE SHORTEST REASONABLE NOTICE.

POSTAL REGULATIONS—(FOREIGN).

RATES OF POSTAGE TO THE FOLLOWING COUNTRIES.

	Letters for every ½ oz. or part of it.	Newspapers for 4 oz. & any adl. 2 oz.	Book Post, 2 oz. or part of it.
To all countries in the British Dominions	2½d.	1d.	1d.
To all Foreign Countries except those mentioned below	4d.	1d.	1d.
Africa, West Coast	9d.	1d.	1d.
Bolivia, (c.) (a.)	1/1	2d.	2d.
Madagascar, (c.)	1/1	2d.	3d.
Chili, Fernando Po	5d.	1d.	1d.
Sandwich Islands	6d.	1d.	1d.
Zanzibar	9d.	1½d.	1½d.
Aden, Borneo, China, Celebes, French Colonies, East of Suez, Japan, Java, Persia Russia, Phillipine Islands, Sumatra	5d.	1½d.	1½d.

N.B.—Registration to all the above countries is 2d. with the exception. of Madagascar to which there is none. (A.) denotes that additional charge will be made on delivery. (C.) denotes that prepayment is compulsory.

PORT-OF-SPAIN, TRAMWAYS.

A Blue and Red Car leave the Railway Station and the Terminus at Tranquility and Belmont at every hour, at twenty minutes after, and 20 minutes before, every hour, commencing at 6.20 a.m. The last car leaves the Railway Station at 9.20 p.m. and Belmont and Tranquillity at 9.40 p.m. The circulating cars leave the Railway Station at 10 minutes *before* and *half past* every *even* hour and 10 minutes *after* every odd hour. From Tranquillity and Belmont the Circulating Cars leave at 10 minutes *after* the even hour and 10 minutes *before* the *odd* hour.

OSBORN'S
Rheumatic Compound.

———:0:0:———

A Certain Cure for Rheumatism.

RHEUMATISM is one of the most painful of maladies, and is unfortunately very common in these climates. Osborn's Rheumatic Compound can however be relied upon to RELIEVE and CURE it :

Try one Bottle and you will add your testimony to that of all who have used it—that it is the CURE FOR RHEUMATIC PAINS of every kind.

TESTIMONIAL:

This is to certify that we the undersigned have used Osborn's Rheumatic Compound and from our experience of its beneficial effects, we have no hesitation in recommending it as a Specific for the Relief and Cure of every description of

Rheumatic Pains.

CHAS. HERISSON, Govt. Printer.
E. M. SOYER, Merchants Clerk.
A. DAVITT, of Cedros.
A. MONDEZIE, of Belmont.
W. LEAGUE, of Arima.
JOHN CLEMENTSON, Sugar Boiler.
LOUIS F. GOMEZ, Clerk.
ALFRED P. MURRAY, Gold Smith.

H. PICHFORD, T. G. R.
W. A. PATRICK, Chaguanas.
HATCHARAN, Contra.
A. FERNANDEZ, East Dry River.
RAMRAITAN MAHARADGE,
                              Chaguanas
SEVERIN MONDESIR, St. Ann's.

N. B.—The original of this Certificate can be examined at the St. James Dispensary, Port-of-Spain, Trinidad.

☞ Sent to any part of the Island by Parcel Post on receipt of Fifty Cents in Postage Stamps, by A. L. INNISS & SON.

TRINIDAD RAILWAY—Time Table.

DOWN.		a. m.	a. m.	*. m.*	p. m.	p. m.	p. m.
Port-of-Spain	—Dep.	7.10	8.30	11.10	* 1.30	4. 0	5.19
San Juan	,,	7.25	8.44	11.25	1.44	4.15	5.33
St. Joseph	,.	7.34	8.52	11.34	1.52	4.24	5.41
Arima Line ⎰ Tunapuna	,,	...	8.59	...	1.59	...	5.48
Tacarigua	,,	...	9. 5	...	2.05	...	5.54
Arouca	,,	...	9.11	...	2.11	...	6. 0
Dabadie	,,	...	9.19	...	2.19	...	6, 8
Arima	—Arr.	...	9.25	...	2.25	...	6.14
Caroni	—Dep.	7.47		11.47		4.37	
Conupia	,,	7.59	...	11.59	...	4.49	...
Chaguanas	,,	8.13	...	12.13	...	5. 3	...
Carapichaima	,,	8.24	...	12.24	...	5.44	...
Couva	,,	8.38	—	12.35	...	5.28	...
California	,,	8.45	...	12.45	...	5.35	...
Claxton Bay	,,	8.57	...	12.57	...	5.47	...
Point-à-Pierre	,,	9. 0	...	1. 0	...	5.50	...
Marbella Junction	,,	9.15	...	1.15	...	6. 5	...
⎰ Union	,,	9.24	...	1.24	...	6.14	...
Williamsville	,,	9.48	...	1.48	...	6.52	...
Princes Town	—Arr.	10. 8	...	2.20	...	7.24	...
San Fernando	,,	9.18	...	1.18	...	6. 8	...
UP.				a. m.*	a. m.	p. m.	p. m.
San Fernando	—Dep.	9. 7	7. 6	1. 5	11. 6	5.57	3.55
⎰ Princes Town	,,	...	6.16	...	10.16	...	2.45
Williamsville	,,	...	6.36	...	10.36	...	3.15
Union	,,	...	7. 0	...	11. 0	...	3.35
Marbella Junction	,,	9.15	7. 9	1.15	11. 9	6. 5	3.58
Princes Town	—Arr.	10. 8	...	2.20	...	7.24	...
Point-à-Pierre	—Dep.		7.14		11.14		4. 3
Claxton Bay	,,	...	7.29	...	11.29	...	4,18
California	,,	...	7.41	...	11.41	...	4.30
Couva	,,	...	7.48	...	11.48	...	4.37
Carapichaima	,,	...	8. 2	...	12. 7	...	4.51
Chaguanas	,,	...	8.13	...	12.13	...	5. 3
Conupia	,,	...	8.28	...	12,28	...	5.17
Caroni	,,		8. 9		12.39		5.28
Arima Line ⎰ Arima	,,	7. 0	...	11. 0	...	3.50	...
Dabadie	,,	7. 7	...	11. 7	...	3.57	...
Arouca	,,	7.15	...	11.15	...	4. 5	...
Tacarigua	,,	7.21	...	11.21	...	4.11	...
Tumpuna	,,	7.27	...	11.27	p. m.	4.17	...
St. Joseph	,,	†7.34	†8.52	†11.34	†12.52	†4.24	†5.41
San Juan	,,	7.43	9. 1	11.43	1. 1	4.23	5.50
Port-of-Spain	—Arr.	7.55	9.13	11.55	1.13	4.45	6. 3

* These trains do not run on Sundays † Passengers from Arima Line for the San Fernando Line change at St. Joseph and vice versa.

Passenger Fares to and from the Principal stations.

	SINGLE. 2 (s. d.)	SINGLE. 3 (s. d.)		SINGLE. 2 (s. d.)	SINGLE. 3 (s. d.)
Port - of - Spain and			**San Fernando and**		
Arima	2 8	1 4	Arima	6 4	3 2
Arouca	2 0	1 0	Arouca	5 10	2 11
Carapichaima	3 4	1 8	California	1 6	0 9
Chaguanas	3 0	1 6	Carapichaima	2 6	1 3
Couva	4 2	2 1	Chaguanas	2 10	1 5
California	4 4	2 2	Claxton Bay	0 10	0 5
Claxton Bay	5 0	2 0	Couva	1 8	0 10
Dabadie	2 4	1 2	Dabadie	6 2	3 1
St. Joseph	1 0	0 6	St. Joseph	4 10	2 5
San Juan	0 8	0 4	San Juan	5 2	2 7
San Fernando	4 2	2 1	Port-of-Spain	4 2	2 1
Point-à-Pierre	5 4	2 8	Point-à-Pierre	0 6	0 3
Princes Town	4 2	2 1	Princes Town	2 0	1 0
Tacarigua	1 8	0 10	Tacarigua	5 6	2 9
Tunapuna	1 4	0 8	Tunapuna	5 2	2 7
Union	4 2	2 1	Union	0 5	0 3
Williamsville	4 2	2 1	Williamsville	1 4	0 8
Couva and Arima	4 10	2 5	**Arima and Arouca**	0 8	0 4
Arouca	4 2	2 1	California	5 0	2 6
California	0 4	0 2	Carapichaima	4 0	2 0
Carapichaima	0 10	0 5	Chaguanas	3 8	1 10
Chaguanas	1 2	0 7	Claxton Bay	5 8	2 10
Claxton Bay	1 0	0 6	Dabadie	0 4	0 2
Dabadie	4 6	2 3	Point-à-Pierre	6 0	3 0
Point-à-Pierre	1 4	0 8	Port-of-Spain	2 8	1 4
Port-of-Spain	4 2	2 1	Princes Town	8 4	4 2
Princes Town	3 8	1 10	St. Joseph	1 8	0 10
St. Joseph	3 2	1 7	San Juan	2 0	1 0
San Juan	3 6	1 9	Tacarigua	1 0	0 6
Tacarigua	3 10	1 11	Tunapuna	1 4	0 8
Tunapuna	3 6	1 9	Union	6 10	3 5
Union	2 2	1 1	Williamsville	7 8	3 10
Williamsville	3 0	1 6	Couva	4 10	2 5
Princestown and Arima	8 4	4 2	**P. Town & Port-of-Spain**	4 2	2 1
Arouca	7 8	3 10	St. Joseph	6 8	3 4
California	3 4	1 8	San Juan	7 0	3 6
Carapichaima	4 14	2 2	Tacarigua	7 4	3 8
Chaguanas	4 10	2 5	Tunapuna	7 0	3 6
Claxton Bay	2 0	1 5	Couva	3 8	1 10
Dabadie	8 0	4 0			

Return Tickets one Fare and a half.

Arnott Lambie & Co.

IRONMONGERS.

Have always on hand a large and varied stock of Mechanics' Tools, Hardware of every description.

CART & BUGGY HARNESS, ETC.

COCOA Bags, Galvanized Buckets, Anchor Chains Ship Scrapers, Pick-axes, Galvanized Iron Riggings, Copper Sheathing, Yellow Metal, Sail Canvas, Window Glass, Nails, &c., &c.

HORSE HIDES.

Carriage Carpets, Carriage Varnishes, Hurricane Lamps, Bass Brooms, Chamois Skins, Electric Bells.

Coach Painters' and Carriage Builders' Materials.

PHOTO. MATERIALS OF ALL KINDS,

All at their acknowledged moderate rates.

Cartridges Loaded to Order.

Cocoa Shipping Agents,

TELEPHONE—No. 133.

Abercrombie Street opposite the Ice [House.

POST OFFICE MONEY ORDERS.

Money Orders may be obtained at the Post Offices in Port-of-Spain, San Fernando, Princes Town, Arima, Couva, Arouca, Chaguanas and Cedros, on each other and on Tobago at the rates in column A. On the United Kingdom, Antigua, Barbados, Demerara, Dominica, Grenada, St. Vincent, St. Lucia, St. Kitts, Montserrat, and Nevis at the rates in column B. On United States of America, Bahamas, Bermuda, Algeria, Australia, Ceylon, Cyprus, Seychelles, Canada, Danish West Indies, Dutch East Indies, Denmark, Egypt, Belgium, France, Gibraltar, Gambia, Gold Coast, Honduras (British), Holland, Falkland Islands, Hong Kong, India (British), Italy, Jamaica, Iceland, Japan, German Empire, Mauritius, North Borneo, Norway, New Zealand, Portugal, Sierra Leone, St. Helena, Straits Settlement, Lagos, Switzerland, Sweden, Turks Island, South Africa and Tasmania at the rates in column C.

No *one* Order will be granted for more than £10 sterling but one person can buy as many £10 Orders as he likes.

No Money Orders are issued at the G.P.O. on the day the English Mail leaves except on Inland Offices.

RATES OF COMMISSION.

	Am't of Order		A.	B.	C.
For any sum not exceeding ...	£	10	2d.	6d.	
„ „ „ ...	1	0	4d.		
„ „ „ ...	2	0		9d.	1/-
„ „ „ ...	2	10	6d.		
„ „ „ ...	5	0	1/-	1/6	2/-
„ „ „ ...	7	0		2/3	3/-
„ „ „ ...	7	10	1/6		
„ „ „ ...	10	0	2/-	3/-	4/-

PUBLIC CART FARES.

1. From the Wharf to any place in a line with King St...15 cents.
2. „ „ „ „ „ „ Duke „ ...20 „
3. „ „ „ „ „ „ The Gaol „ ...25 „

PORTERS.

1. For the day ... ... 60 cents.
2. „ half day ... ... 40 „
3. „ the hour ... ... 15 „
4. „ the trip or job ... ... 10 „

Savings Bank.

The Government Savings Bank at the Treasury. Port-of-Spain and the Branch Savings Banks at San Fernando, Arima, St. Joseph, Couva, Tortuga, Princes Town, Cedros, Moruga and Mayaro, receive deposits at interest. The interest is 3 per cent. per annum. Fractions of a shilling are not received and no interest is paid on parts of a Pound Sterling or for any time less than one month, nor on deposits exceeding £200. Deposits may be made by and repaid to infants. Married women may withdraw their deposits without the signature of husbands. Upon the death of a depositor the amount of his or her deposit may be paid to the person appointed in the manner prescribed by the Savings Banks Ordinance 1882 and when there is no such appointment then to the person entitled to the personal estate of the deceased depositor.

Penny Savings Bank.

There are in Port-of-Spain 5 Penny Savings Banks in which sums from 1 penny upwards can be deposited. No interest is given on these deposits. The hours when these Penny Banks are opened are as follows:

Greyfriars at Brunswick Square on Mondays from 7 to 8 p.m
Belmont at Anglican School-house ,, Wednesdays ,, 7 to 9 ,,
Wesleyan at Hanover street ,, Fridays ,, 5 to 6 ,,
Free Church at St. Ann's Road ,, Saturdays ,, 7 to 8 ,,
St John's at Pembroke street ,, Mondays from 6.30 to 7.30 ,,
In San Fernando there is also a Penny Savings Bank in connection with the Susamachar Church on Wednesdays from 5.45 to 6.45 p.m.

Colonial Hospital.

Visiting days for Patients' friends : Mondays, Tuesdays, Fridays and Saturdays from 12 to 1 p.m. by Ticket obtainable at the gate.

Census Returns.

Port-of-Spain	...	33,782	San Fernando	...	6,633
St. Ann's Ward Union	...	16,170	Naparima Ward Union	...	27,512
Diego Martin ,,	,,	12,015	Savana Grande ,,	,,	17,505
Tacarigua ,,	,,	15,508	Mayaro ,,	,,	2,327
Arima ,,	,,	14,321	Cedros ,,	,,	5,794
Couva ,,	,,	13,662	Toco ,,	,,	2,797
Chaguanas ,,	,,	10,140	Blanchisseuse Ward	...	744
Montserrat ,,	,,	10,874	Grand Total ...		199,784

Cab Fares, Port-of-Spain.

Between the following Places.	Fountain King St.		Railway Station		St. Vincent Jetty		Park St. West end		Park St. East End		Botanic Garden	
	s.	d.	s.	d.	s.	d.	s.	d.	s.	d.	s.	d.
St. James Barracks	2	6	2	6	2	6	1	6	1	9	......	
Botanic Gardens	1	9	1	9	1	9	1	6	1	3	......	
Royal Gaol	1	0	1	0	1	0	1	0	1	0	1	3
Government and Court Houses	1	0	1	0	1	0	1	0	1	0	1	6
Colonial Hospital	1	0	1	0	1	0	1	0	1	0	1	0
King Street Fountain	......		1	0	1	0	1	0	1	0	1	9
St. Vincent Wharf and Jetty	1	0	1	0	......		1	0	1	0	1	9
Lunatic Asylum	2	0	2	0	2	0	1	9	1	3	1	0
Park Street, West end	1	0	1	0	1	0	......		1	0	1	6
" " East end	1	0	1	0	1	0	1	0	......		1	3
Barrack Street	1	0	1	0	1	0	1	0	1	0	1	0
Queen's Park, N. W. corner	2	0	2	0	2	0	1	3	1	6	1	0
" " S. W. corner	1	6	1	6	1	6	1	0	1	0	1	3
Railway Station	1	0	......		1	0	1	0	1	0	1	9
Woodbrook	1	3	1	6	1	3	1	0	1	0	1	3
Woodford Street, North end	1	6	1	6	1	6	1	0	1	3	1	0

	s.	d.
From Fountain to St. Ann's Police Station	2	3
" " Round Circular Road and back	4	3
Circular Road round Queen's Park	2	3
Fares by time. For any time not exceeding one hour	4	0
For every subsequent quarter of an hour	0	9
Fares by distance. Any distance not exceeding one mile	1	0
For every quarter of a mile beyond	0	3

Boat Fares.

	s.	d.
To and from any Vessel lying ¼ mile from shore with 1 or 2 passengers	1	0
Every additional passenger	0	6
To and from any Vessel lying not more than a mile	2	0
Every additional passenger	1	0
For Vessels lying beyond a mile, for every additional ¼ mile	1	0
Additional for every passenger beyond 2	1	6
One package free of charge, for every additional pkge.	0	3

Alfred Richards & Co.

Wholesale & Retail

PHARMACISTS & DRUGGISTS,

THE PHŒNIX PHARMACY,

No, 34A, King Street—Port-of-Spain,

TRINIDAD.

PRESCRIPTIONS ACCURATELY COMPOUNDED,
COPIED AND RETURNED.

Every Article of the Best Description.

PHYSICIANS' PRESCRIPTIONS

AND

FAMILY RECIPES

CAREFULLY COMPOUNDED BY COMPETENT LICENSED

DRUGGISTS,

At all Hours Day and Night.

WITH THE PUREST DRUGS.

——:o:o:——

TOILET ARTICLES

OF EVERY DESCRIPTION ON HAND AND AT PRICES
TO SUIT ALL.

IMPORT DUTIES.

Bread of all kinds	90lbs the barrel ...		1	6
Butter	the lb. ...	0	0	1
Oleomargarine, Butterine, or any preparation of fat other than Lard or Ghee...	the lb ...	0	0	1
Carriages on Spring, four-wheeled	each ...	7	0	0
„ „ two -wheeld	each ...	4	0	0
Cheese	the lb. ...	0	0	1
Corn of all kinds including Oats ...	the bushel ...	0	0	5
Dogs	each ...	0	10	0
Flour	the barrel of 196 lbs. ...	0	3	4
Gunpowder	the lb. ...	0	0	7
Ghee	the lb. ...	0	0	1
Hardware, for every £100 of value	... ...	4	0	0
Earthen and Glassware, for every £100 of value	... ...	4	0	0
Furniture, for every £100 of value	... ...	4	0	0
Lard	the 100 lb ...	0	3	0
Leather manufactures, for every £100 of value...	... ...	4	0	0

Liquors, viz.:

Malt Liquor, in wood ...	the gallon... ...	0	0	6
„ in bottles, the dozen reputed quart bottles and so in proportion ...	... ...	0	1	0
Rum—for every gallon of the strength of proof as ascertained by Sykes' hydrometer, and so in proportion for any greater or less strength than the strength of proof & for any greater or less quantity than a gallon	the gallon ...	0	6	6
Methylated Spirits, admitted as such by the Collector of Customs...	... the gallon ...	0	1	6
All other Spirits. Strong Waters, Liqueurs and Cordials, if not exceeding the strength of proof as ascertained by Sykes' hydrometer, except Tinctures by	... the liquid gallon ...	0	9	0

And for every degree of strength beyond that specified above an additional duty of one penny the liquid gallon.

Wines in Bottle.				
Sparkling Wines	the gallon ...	0	4	0
All other Wines in bottle containing less than the following rates of proof spirit as verified by Sykes' hydrometer, at 42 degrees ...	the gallon ...	0	2	6

And for every degree of strength beyond that above specified an additional duty of threepence per gallon.

(Continued on page 53.).

Wines in Wood.

For all Wines in Wood containing less than the following rates of proof spirit as verified by Sykes' hydrometer. viz. :

22 degrees	...	...	...	the gallon ...	0	0	8
32 degrees	...	...	...	the gallon ...	0	1	0
42 degrees	..	...	...	the gallon ...	0	2	6

And for every degree of strength beyond the highest above specified an additional duty of threepence per gallon

Matches, Lucifer, for every gross of boxes or other packages, each box or package containing not more than 120 matches, if containing more than 120 matches, duty to be charged in proportion	0	2	6
Meal or other Flour not Wheaten ... the barrel ...	0	2	0
Muskets, Guns, Pistols, Fowling Pieces, Gun Barrels, and Gun Stocks ... ... each ...	0	5	0
Oil—Creosote, for every £100 of value	4	0	0
Coconut ... ... the gallon ...	0	1	0
Petroleum ... ... the gallon ...	0	1	0
All other kinds ... ... the gallon ...	0	1	0
Oil Meal ... ... the 100 lb. ...	0	1	0
Opium—including all goods, wares, or merchandize mixed or saturated with opium or with any preparation thereof, except tincture of opium, admitted by the Collector of Customs as being for medicinal purposes only, which shall be charged with duty at the rate payable by goods unenumerated, the lb. ...	0	10	0
Rice ... ... the 100 lb. ...	0	2	2
Soap ... ... the 100 lb. ...	0	2	1
Sugar ... ... the 100 lb. ...	0	10	0
Tea ... ... the lb. ...	0	0	6
Timber—Sawn or hewn ...the 1000 feet superficial ...	0	8	3
Shingles ... ... the 1000 ...	0	1	6
Shooks ... ... the bundle ...	0	0	7
Staves ... ... the 1000 ...	0	12	0
Wood Hoops ... ... the 1000 ...	0	3	0
Tobacco—Unmanufactured... ... the lb. ...	0	1	0
Cigars and Cigarettes ... the lb. ...	0	3	0
All other manufactured Tobacco the lb. ...	0	1	4
Textile Manufactures of all kinds, Wearing Apparel of all kinds, Haberdashery, for every £100 of value ...	4	0	0
All other goods, wares, merchandise and effects of every description not previously enumerated, ... for every £100 of value ...	4	0	0

MEDICAL HALL—The oldest established Drug Shop in the Colony.

MEDICAL HALL—For Prescriptions and all kinds of Medicines.

MEDICAL HALL—For Perfumes, Soaps, and all Toilet Requisites.

MEDICAL HALL—Depôt for Mother Payne's Tetter Cure.

MEDICAL HALL—A full line of Groceries and Wines.

MEDICAL HALL—For School Books—every sort.

MEDICAL HALL—For School Requisites, all that may be required.

MEDICAL HALL—A full line of Stationeries.

J. C. Newbold & Co.

No. 2, Marine Square, Port-of-Spain.

LUMBER MERCHANTS

HAVE ALWAYS ON HAND

Galvanized. Sheets, Cement,

Hinges, Nails, Bricks,

Lime, Locks, &c.

GULF STEAMERS.

SAN FERNANDO AND CEDROS SERVICE—Time Table.

TUESDAY—Leave Sanfernando at 7 a.m.—Arrive Port-of-Spain, at 10 p.m ; Leave Port-of-Spain at 4 p.m. ; Arrive Sanfernando at 7 p.m.

WEDNESDAY—Leave Sanfernando at 9:30 a m.—Arrive Cedros at 12:45 p. m.—Leave Cedros at 1 p.m. Arrive Sanfernando at 4:15 p. m. ; Port-of-Spain 7.15 p. m.

FRIDAY—Leave Port-of-Spain at 7 a. m. ; Leave Sanfernando at 10 a.m. ; Arrive Cedros at 1.15 p.m. ; Leave Cedros at 1:30 p. m. ; Arrive Sanfernando at 5:45 ; Port-of-Spain at 7:45.

PORT OF SPAIN AND MONOS SERVICE—Time Table.

MONDAY—Leave Port-of-Spain at 5 a. m.—Leave Monos at 7 a.m.—Arrive Port-of-Spain at 9:30 a. m.—Leave Port-of-Spain at 2 p m.—Arrive Monos at 4:30 p. m.

THURSDAY—Leave Port-of-Spain at 8 a. m.—Arrive Chacachacare at 11:30 a. m.—Leave Chacachacare at 2:30 p. m.—Arrive Port-of-Spain at 6 p. m.

SATURDAY—Leave Port-of-Spain at 5 a. m.—Leave Monos at 7 a.m.—Arrive Port-of-Spain at 9:30 a. m.—Leave Port-of-Spain at 1 p.m.—Arrive Monos at 3:30—Leave Monos at 4 p. m.—Arrive Port-of-Spain at 6 p.m.

Fares to and from Port of Spain.

		CABIN.			STEERAGE.	
		S.	R.		S.	R.
Carenage	...	48c.	72c. ...	...	24c.	36c.
Five Islands	...	48c.	72c. ...	...	24c.	36c.
Gasparee	...	72c.	$1 08 ...	...	36c.	54c.
Monos	...	96c.	$1 44 ...	...	48c.	72c.

Return Tickets available on day of issue only, or if issued on Saturday till Monday.

ALEXANDER DÉCLE, Senior,

WATCHMAKER, JEWELLER, &c,

No. 29. FREDERICK STREET.

Gold and Silver WATCHES. **Gold and Silver CHAINS.**

American CLOCKS.

French & English Jewellery of the Richest & most Elegant Designs.

SOLE AGENT FOR THE Alaska Pebbles Perfected Spectacles and Glasses.

Also other SPECTACLES AND GOGGLES in Great Variety.

Chronometers rated and repaired. Watches, Clocks and Musical Boxes Cleaned and repaired.

Clocks Wound up and kept in Order by the Year.

Jewellery, Etc., Repaired. Electro-Plating & Gilding in the most recent Fashions.

——(:o:o:)——

PORT-OF-SPAIN, TRINIDAD.

Charles Hales,

MANUFACTURER OF

Brown, Blue and Mottled Soaps

AT THE

Pioneer Soap Works.

MANUFACTURER OF

PURE COCONUT OIL

AT THE

Central Coconut Oil Works,

LA BASSE PORT-OF-SPAIN.

STEAM SERVICE ROUND THE ISLAND AND TOBAGO
RATES OF PASSAGE.

The Steamer leaves Port-of-Spain every Tuesday by the Northern and Southern Routes alternately, but touches at Tobago only every two weeks.

From	1st Class.		2nd Class		Deck.
	N.	S.	N.	S.	N. or S.
	$	$	$	$	$
Port-of-Spain to or from Blanchisseuse ...	3 00	8 00	2 00	4 00	1 44
,, ,, Toco ...	4 00	7 00	2 00	4 00	,,
,, ,, Salibea ...	6 00	7 00	3 00	3 00	,,
,, ,, Manzanilla ...	6 00	6 00	3 00	3 00	,,
,, ,, Mayaro ...	6 00	6 00	3 00	3 00	,,
,, ,, Guayaguayare ...	7 00	5 00	4 00	3 00	,,
,, ,, Moruga ...	7 00	4 00	4 00	2 00	,,
,, ,, Erin ...	7 00	4 00	4 00	2 00	,,
,, ,, Hicacos ...	8 00	3 00	4 00	2 00	,,
,, ,, Tobago ...	6 00	9 00	3 00	5 00	,,
To or from Intermediate Stations ...	1 44	1 44	0 96	0 96	0 72

Meals not included in the above rates.

Excursion and Return Tickets 1st class between Port-of-Spain and Tobago (for one month) $10 North or South.

Nurses and Servants accompanying their Employers and travelling cabin, pay two-thirds cabin rate, children up to 9 years of age half fare, infants in arms free—passengers luggage to the extent of 10 cubic feet, free, anything in excess will be charged extra. All passengers must embark and land at their own expense, or if landed by the Steamer a charge of one shilling each will be made.

SAN FERNANDO BOAT FARES.

For any distance not exceeding 500 yards, each passenger, 12½ cents
Beyond 500 yards and not exceeding 1 mile ,, ,, 25 ,,
For every additional mile beyond the the first for any number
    of passengers not exceeding four ... ... 25 ,,

New American Soda Water Factory.
25A, UPPER PRINCE STREET. 25A.

THE PROPRIETOR

of the above establishment has the pleasure to inform the public that he has recently imported from the celebrated house of HERMANN, LACHAPELLE & Co., of Paris, one of their latest and most approved

Machines, FITTED UP WITH ONE OF Pasteur's Filters,

the only one in use in a Soda Water Factory in Trinidad.

Previous to the importation of the new plant of machinery, the water used in manufacturing beverages at the NEW AMERICAN SODA WATER FACTORY was filtered through a Carbon Filter, the use of which is still retained. It will therefore be seen that at present *A DOUBLE GUARANTEE OF PURITY* is offered, and the products of the Factory are exceptional from a sanitary point of view.

A list of the various Aerated Beverages always on hand is appended, and special orders for new varieties will be undertaken

SODA WATER	LEMON	NECTAR
GINGER ALE	RASPBERRY	ETC., ETC.,
VANILLA	PEARS	ETC., ETC.

The attention of the public is also drawn to the subjoined certificate from the Government Analyst :—

I hereby certify that the sample of Aerated Water received on the 23rd July 1891 from the New American Soda Water Foctory has been analysed by me with the following results :—

The water is well aerated and of first class commercial quality. It has evidently been carefully prepared as it is free from deleterious ingredients, and I can therefore safely recommend it for use.

The samples of Lemonade and Ginger Ale submitted by the same firm show the same care in preparation. They possess a very agreeable taste and flavour.

(Signed) P. CARMODY, F.L.C., E.C.S., &c.,
Government Analyst and Professor of Chemistry
to the Royal and St. Mary's Colleges.
Government Laboratory. Port-of-Spain, Trinidad,

The Proprietor, while thanking the public for the patronage already generously extended to him, would solicit further orders, whether wholesale or retail, for the execution of which he guarantees *despatch and satisfaction to his customers.*

Chief Officers of the Government.

SALARIES.

Gavernor—Sir Frederick Napier Broome, K.C.M.G. ...	£5000
Colonial Secretary—Henry Fowler	1000
Assistant Colonial Secretary—A. C. Ross	600
Chief Clerk—J. Cunningham	450
Auditor-General—H. W. Chantrell	850
First Clerk—E. Eckle	450
Director of Public Works and Railway—J. E. Tanner (for	
Railway £500)	1700
Assistant Director of Public Works	950
Assistant Engineer—P. Stevens...	650
Financial Assistant—R. F. Smith	400
Protector of Immigrants—C. Mitchell...	800
Sub-Protector and Inspector of Immigrants —H. C. Stone ...	450
Senior Assistant Protector of Immigrants—H. G. Pasea ...	400
Junior Assistant Protector of Immigrants—F. J. Gibbon ...	360
First Clerk—N. A. St. Hillaire...	350
Chief Interpreter—J. C. McHugh	300
Receiver-General—C. B. Hamilton	800
Sub-Receiver—O. FitzGerald	400
Accountant—Clarence Ross	450
Cashier—J. Brown	400
Excise Officer—C. W. Langford	400
Supervisor—G. W. Norman, Jnr.	400
Collector of Customs—J. Fanning	800
Chief Clerk—C. Farnum...	450
Second Clerk—H. Wainwright	300
Principal Landing Waiter—F. B. Fraser	350
First Class Landing Waiter—A. Hart...	300
Registrar-General—D. B. Horsford	800
Deputy Registrar-General—E. C. M. Stone	400
Examiner of Titles—G. L. Garcia, Q.C.	700
Harbour Master—G. W. Norman	500
Assistant Harbour Master—R. C. Rochford	250
Postmaster General—J. A. Bulmer	550
Chief Clerk—J. Norman	220
Postmaster San Fernando—J. C. Lewis	300
Sub-Intendant Crown Lands—D. Wilson	1,000
Assistant Sub-Intendant Crown Lands—G. F. Bushe ...	400
Engineer of Surveys—C. S. Cochrane	600
First Assistant Surveyor—H. de Lapeyruse	400
Second Assistant Surveyor—J. E. Morvant	350
Third Assistant Surveyor—R. Kernahan	300
Superintendent Botanic Gardens—J. H. Hart, F.L.S. ...	425

(Continued on page 61.)

JAMES SKEOCH,
Dry Goods Merchant

FOR BEST VALUE AND BEST ASSORTED STOCK IN

FANCY & STAPLE DRY GOODS,

FLOWERS,   FEATHERS,

HATS,

Gloves, Ribbons, Silks, &c., &c., &c.,

GO TO

THE TRINIDAD EMPORIUM,

5a, Frederick Street.

WESTERN FIRE ASSURANCE Co.

——:o:o:——

Lowest Rates of any company doing business
in the Island.

Losses Settled with promptness and liberality.

☞ NOTE.—New three-year rates on private residences
effect a saving of 25 per cent.

JAMES SKEOCH, AGENT.

5A, Frederick-street.

Assistant Supt, Botanic Gardens—W. E. Broadway	145
Superintendant of Pastures and Examiner of Animals —J. B. White	550
Superintendent of Government Printing Office—H. J. Clark	600
Chief Justice—Sir John Gorrie, Kt.	1,800
First Puisne Judge—John Cook	1,000
Second Puisne Judge—Chas. F. Lumb	1,000
Registrar of the Courts and Marshal—Chas. H. Philips	800
Chief Clerk—E. D. Clarke	300
Attorney General—S. H. Gatty, Q.C.	1,000
Solicitor General and Law Officer for Tobago—G. L. Garcia, Q.C.	450
Crown Solicitor—L. D. O'Connor	300
Assistant Marshal—D. Hart	250
Inspector of Schools—R. G. Bushe	700
First Assistant Inspector of Schools—W. H. Robinson	275
Second Assistant Inspector of Schools—C. H. D. Hobson	200
Third Assistant Inspector of Schools—E. G. Peñalosa	200
Accountant—A. E. Brereton	200
Superintendent Boys' Model School—J. H. Collens	400
Superintendent Girls' Model School—H. Bowen	250
Principal Queen's Royal College—W. Miles	700
Second Master—Burslum	500
Third Master—C. Bishop	400
Professor Chemistry and Government Analyst—P. Carmody	600
French and Spanish Master—C. Bradshaw	250
Professor St. Mary's College—Rev. J. Browne	500
Surgeon General—S. L. Crane, C.M.G.	1,000
Chief Clerk—	325
Sanitary Inspector and Sec'tary Board of Health—F. J. Fuller	350
Dispenser Colonial Hospital—J. B. Inniss	200
Dispenser San Fernando Hospital—J. E. Samuels	150
Inspector General of Police and Captain of Fire Brigade— Captain E. Fortescue	1,000
Inspector of Southern Division—A. D. P. Owen	625
Inspector of Northern Division—J. Brierly	420
Sub-Inspector—J. Giblan	262
Superintendant of Prisons—L. M. Fraser	500
First Clerk—G. F. Bourne	230
Superintendant Convict Depot—Chas. W. Meaden	300
Railway Traffic Manager—A. R Gray	550
Assistant Traffic Manager—F. J. Mahoney	310
First Clerk and Accountant—J. H. King	205
Locomotive Engineer—J. W. Tomlinson	400
Engineer—F. Labastide	300
Assistant Engineer—Albert Labastide	210
Commandant Volunteers—Col. Mann	650

(Continued on page 63.)

TAITT & SON,

Chemists and Druggists,

CORNER FREDERICK AND QUEEN STREETS.

PRSECRIPTIONS

From any country and any kind made up with accuracy, and with
the best drugs, both day and night.

Agents for the World Renowned

Dr. KILMER'S MEDICINES,

AS WELL AS FOR

AYER & CO.

EVERYTHING FOR THE TOILET!

ALL PATENT MEDICINES,

63

STIPENDIARY MAGISTRATES.

Port-of-Spain and Western District of County of St. George—W. L. Lewis	£750
St. George County East—O. Harley	600
San Fernando and Victoria County—Rayner	600
Savana Grande and Moruga—H. P. Hobson	650
Cedros and Warden—A. C. Newsam	675
Caroni and Warden—J. A. Harrigan	900
Arima and Blanchisseuse and Warden—L. P. Pierre	650
Mayaro and Warden—H. D. Huggins	500
Toco and Warden—J. F. Redhead	450
Oropouche, La Brea and Erin and Warden—M. T. Pasea	325

WARDENS.

Arima—G. F. R. H. Harrigan	475
Montserrat—C. Flanagan	350
Tacarigua—T. H. Warner	400
Chaguanas and Couva—W. L. Lacroix	400
St Ann's and Diego Martin—A. S. Bowen	300
Naparima—R. Johnston	500
Savana Grande—H. C. Warner	425
Oropouche—T. Pasea	325

TOBAGO.

Commissioner and Treasurer and Comptroller of Customs—His Honor L. G. Hay	£600
Stipendiary J.P., Coroner of the Leward District and Commissioner of Supreme Court—S. J. Fraser	400
Stipendiary J.P., and Coroner of the Winward District—Thos. N. Brown	320
Inspector of Police and Superintendent of Excise and Marshal of Prison—W. Pasea	350
Registrar Supreme Court and Auditor—Robert H. Sealy	250
Postmaster and Chief Clerk of Treasurer—A. L. Marshall	180
Colonial Surgeon and Medical Officer for the Leward District—J. P. Tulloch	300
Medical Officer for the Winward District—E. G. Blanc	200
Medical Officer for the Northern District—W. Norman	200
Commissioner of Roads—Edward McDougall	90
Harbour Master and Chief Landing Waiter—Q. H. Spicer (fees) &	90

EXPORTS OF 1890.

Sugar—53,813 tons; Cocoa—21,552,595 lbs. or 124,665 bags; Molasses 2,024,834 gallons; Rum—284,999 gallons.
Asphalt, Raw—68,201 tons; Asphalt Epuré—21,280 tons; Coconuts—12,739,904; Bitters—43,466 gallons.

TOBAGO.

Sugar—1,129 tons; Molasses—405 puncheons; Coconuts—524,312

RAILWAYS AND ROADS.

Railways, 54½ miles ; Metalled Roads, 117 miles ; Gravelled Roads, 126½ miles ; Natural Soil Roads, 324 miles ; Bridle Roads 471½ miles.

Number of Steamers entered at Trinidad in 1890, 493. Tonnage 535,386,493.

Number of Sailing Vessels entered at Trinidad in 1890, 505. Tonnage —552,146,505.

Revenue of Trinidad for 1890 ... £468.559
Expenditure of Trinidad for 1890 ... 475,244 Public Debt £532,000.

Revenue of Tobago for 1890 ... £8.656
Expenditure of Tobago for 1890 ... 9,256 Public Debt £5,000.

Number of Children in School in Trinidad, 19,685. Tobago 2.580.
Revenue from Pitch Lake in 1890... ... ... £26,744.
Value of Imports 1890, £951,695 ;

ESTATES IN TOBAGO.

Steam 19 ; Steam and Water 2 ; Wind 6 ; Water 3 ; Cattle 2—To'tl 32.

DISPENSING DEPARTMENT.

TO THE MEDICAL PROFESSION.

VOICE "TABLOIDS"—*Composed of* COCAINE, *Chlorate of Potash and Borax.* Impart a clear and silvery tone to the voice. Easily retained in the mouth while singing or speaking. Now used by the leading singers and public speakers throughout the world.

DIRECTIONS.—A single "Tabloid" may be slowly dissolved in the mouth to remove huskiness or hoarseness.

TOILET "LANOLINE"—"*Lanoline*" is emollient, protective and soothing. it supplies the skin with a "cream" natural to it, and is highly regarded for abrasions, chapped hands roughness, hardness, etc.

"Possesses remarkable properties in the prevention of sun burn and freckles."—*British Medical Journal.*

"LANOLINE" TOILET SOAP.— THE NATURAL SKIN SOAP.

"*Lanoline*" is acknowleged by dermatologists to be the very best preservative of the skin, restoring its soft, pliable and elastic nature, and healthful surface.

"The Soap for delicate skins."—*Edinburgh Medical Journal.*

THE PATENT THERMO-SAFEGUARD FEEDING BOTTLE.—

Is the safest and most perfect in existence and enables the nurse to ascertain at all times the quantity and temperature of the food given.

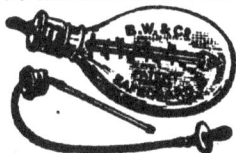

"The bottle has a great deal to recommend it" —*British Medical Journal.*

"The best of all feeding bottles and ought to be universally used."—*Edin. Medical Journal,* Supplied in three sizes.

ZYMINE PEPTONISING POWDERS (Fairchild).—One tube added to a pint of cows' milk so predigests it that it will no longer form a curd to irritate and inflame the infant or invalid stomach. They render cows' milk precisely like mothers' milk. "The introduction of which has probably done more than any other therapeutic measure of recent times to lessen infant mortality.—*British Medical Journnl.* Admirably adapted for use with the Thermo-Safeguard Feeding Bottle. Supplied in boxes containing one dozen tubes,

KEPLER SOLUTION OF COD LIVER OIL IN MALT EXTRACT

—"Taste of the oil agreeably disguised, its nutritive powers greatly increased and it is rendered easy of digestion.—*British Medical Journal.*

Patients grow fat upon it when other forms of oil cause distress and pain.

KEPLER EXTRACT OF MALT.—A delicious concentrated, nutritious, digestive food for dyspeptics, invalids and infants. *The Lancet* says : "It is the best and most largely used." The consumptive's best resort. It is the best substitute for cod liver oil.

BURROUGHS WELCOME & Co., SNOW HILL BUILDINGS, London.

CARIBBEAN SEA

THE ISLAND OF TRINIDAD

GULF OF PARIA

ATLANTIC OCEAN